BE MORE WITCH

ALISON DAVIES

Illustrations by Megan Reddi

Hardie Grant

QUADRILLE

CONTENTS

INTRODUCTION

If the broom fits, ride it – or so they say, and I have always felt a kinship with the way of the witch. Whether mistresses of the Moon, wild women of the woods or the gentle weavers of fate, the modern enchantress can be all this and more. The world is her cauldron; a giant, bubbling pot of ideas, energy and enthusiasm, from which she can draw potential and create her own magical path. Today's witch has no limits, unlike her sisters that went before. She is not held back by prejudice or the weight of her crumpled cloak. Neither does she suffer such fashion blunders as the pointy, misshapen hat, worn at a jaunty angle. The only labels she wears are designer, and of her choosing.

Adept in the art of spellcasting, she'll conjure on the move, at her desk, or lunching with the girls, because she is the magic. A fairy-tale princess might favour the prince who comes to her rescue, but the feisty witch sorts it herself, saving face and the day, and all before breakfast.

Taking strength from the old ways, and using Mother Nature as the ultimate inspiring meme, it's no wonder witches fly high, and you can too. Whether you have a whimsical interest in the craft or want to go the whole Halloween-style hog, here is where you dip your wand in the water! Each chapter covers a different aspect of witchiness and shows how, with a little effort and intention, you can conjure magic every day. From getting your mystical mojo on, to sharing the love and making intuition your new BFF, it's a simple process; be witch to bewitch. Let the enchantment begin!

'I think all women are witches, in the sense that a witch is a magical being.'

YOKO ONO

Witches make things happen. 'Seize the day,' is their motto of choice, swiftly followed by 'if at first you don't succeed, try, try, try again.' Where there's a witch, there's almost certainly a way. And not just one way, thousands of magical and effective ways to make anything happen, so if you think that witchcraft is a dark and sombre practice involving cauldrons, frog's legs, and lots of black, think again!

Gone are the warty-nosed hags of old, the traditional and mean-spirited image so often portrayed in fairy tales. In its place you'll find sass with a capital 'S'. These ladies may or may not wield wands (a matter of personal choice), but they do brandish words and thoughts. They match action with intention and a positive outlook to make waves. Like the word itself, which comes from the Old English 'wicce' meaning 'female witch', and has its roots in the Anglo-Saxon term 'wic', which means 'to bend or twist', a witch transforms things! From her personal thoughts, to how she looks, feels and behaves, she rings in the changes. This in turn causes an external reaction and a positive outcome. Easy as saying, 'Hocus-pocus!'

Ultimately, witches take the power back. They don't bemoan their fate. Neither do they turn a blind eye, or stick their head in the sand. A witch is a warrior of sorts. She sets trends, believes in magic and follows her heart in all things. An approach no doubt influenced by the witch trials that saw many innocent men, women and children slaughtered during the Middle Ages. Being different meant being vilified. Even something as simple as being unmarried or helping to heal a sick neighbour was enough to qualify you as a cohort of the devil. Luckily attitudes have changed, but witches remain resolute. They think smart! Whatever they want they create through thought, word and deed. Simple as!

WITCHY WAYS
TO THINK SMART

👁 Silence the critic. When you hear your inner voice saying something negative, shout, 'Stop!' in your head, and replace it with something positive.

👁 Repeat positive affirmations to reprogramme your thoughts, things like, 'I am loved', 'Today is magical', or 'I love life'. These magical phrases lift the spirits and encourage happy thoughts.

👁 Feeling anxious? Focus on your breathing and imagine you're cocooned in bright white light. You should feel instantly protected, and more positive.

👁 Make the day magic by stating what you'd like to happen, for example: 'Today everything I touch turns to gold. I impress my boss and get a promotion. I have fun with my work colleagues and a lovely relaxing evening with my other half'.

BE MORE WITCH

If you're using thoughts and affirmations in a magical way to manifest the things you'd like to happen, keep them in the present tense, so say, 'I am/have' rather than, 'I will be/will have', as this places them in the future and out of reach.

'You have to believe
in yourself.'

DEBBIE REYNOLDS

Athletes picture success. They see the finishing line, imagine crossing it and hold that feeling in their heart until it happens for real. Witches do the same. They know a picture speaks a thousand words, and while the right ingredients and actions help, being able to visualise your desired outcome is the icing on the cake.

Try this:

✧ Think of something you'd like. Go for something small and then build up to the bigger stuff – so you might be looking for the perfect pair of shoes to match an outfit, at a snip of a price.

✧ Close your eyes and picture the shoes. Include lots of detail and an affordable price tag.

✧ Now picture yourself out shopping. You see the shoes and they're within your budget. You try them on and they look and feel fabulous.

✧ Finally see yourself buying the shoes and returning home with your prize!

✧ Repeat the visualisation every day for a week for swift results.

BE MORE WITCH

Make visualisations real and effective,
by engaging your emotions. Think how
you'll feel when you achieve your dream
and conjure up those emotions.

GO WITH THE
MYSTICAL FLOW.

'The Moon has awoken, with the sleep of the Sun, the light has been broken, the spell has begun.'

MIDGARD MORNINGSTAR

TAIRRIE B. MURPHY (CARPE NOCTEM / VINTAGE CURSES)

THE MAGIC OF SPELLS

Spells come in all shapes and sizes, and that's what makes them unique, personal and ultra-powerful. Like your mum's homemade stew, with that secret ingredient she'll never reveal, it's a recipe of sorts; a set of ingredients, a few charmed words and an intention to satisfy. Spells can be fun too, a light-hearted way of providing focus and helping you look to the future with optimism. It's easy to obsess over what we think we need and limit ourselves in the process. Spells help us detach. We make a wish. We put it out there. We get on with life and go with the mystical flow. What's not to love?

THINGS TO KNOW
ABOUT SPELLS

✧ You must be in the right frame of mind. You may be fed up with flings and looking for love, but if you're in a foul mood, then your spell will fall foul too.

✧ You can't change free will. You might have the hots for the guy you see at the coffee shop every morning, but you can't make him love you if his heart is set on another.

✧ Spells are simple. You only need three things, your intention (to attract a cash windfall), an action (lighting a candle/burning some incense) and your will (the positive energy you put into it when you make your wish).

'The world is full of magic things, patiently waiting for our senses to grow sharper.'

W.B.YEATS

WITCH'S TOOLKIT ESSENTIALS

Wand
Wave it like
you mean it!

Candles
Light to create a
magical atmosphere

Cauldron
Stir and focus
while it bubbles

Crystal Ball
Gaze and let
your mind wander

Magic Mirror
Ideal for perfecting
your witchy stare!

Book of Shadows
A fancy notebook for
jotting down spells

Kit sorted, check! Frame of mind positive, check! It's
time to get your mojo on. These simple spells are based
on ancient rituals. Practise, adapt or make up your own.
There are no rules in Witch School, so enjoy!

SPELL TO REVEAL YOUR TRUE LOVE

Every good witch knows the secret to romance is an open heart and mind, but if you're itching to discover your ideal match, or you just want to attract love fast, this spell is for you.

You will need: a knife; a red apple; a tissue.

1 Cut the apple into two halves to represent you and your beloved.

2 Remove the seeds and wrap them in a tissue.

3 Place under your pillow while saying, 'True love so sweet, I am ready to meet. From this moment in time, may your heart beat with mine'.

4 Your potential love interest could show up in your dreams, but if not, remove the seeds the next day and scatter outside, while repeating the magical chant to draw them into your life.

BE MORE WITCH

Love yourself. When you truly love who
you are and the life you have created,
then love will ALWAYS find you!

LADY LUCK GOOD FORTUNE SPELL

Make friends with Lady Luck and make every day count!

You will need: cinnamon powder; nutmeg powder.

1 Cinnamon powder is associated with success and nutmeg is known as the gambler's spice. Combine a teaspoon of each into a powder.

2 Dust over your palms, then clasp them together. Say, 'Lady luck is in my grasp. Good fortune is here and set to last'.

3 Rinse your hands in warm water and repeat the magical chant while picturing a rainbow of light above your head.

BE MORE WITCH

Try carrying a whole nutmeg in your pocket. According to folklore this attracts good luck!

MAKE ME A MONEY MAGNET SPELL

While you may not win a million, this spell will give your piggy bank a boost and get the cash rolling in.

You will need: a magnet; a clean jar; loose change.

1 Pop the magnet inside the jar – a fridge magnet is fine for this. Then search your purse, pockets and drawers for loose change and drop it in.

2 As you do this say, 'Coppers, coins and all that cash, are drawn to me, in a flash!'

3 Every day shake the jar and repeat the phrase.

4 Keep adding any spare change you find over the next couple of weeks.

5 At the end of this time, not only will you have the stash of cash you've collected, you should also receive a surprise windfall.

BE MORE WITCH

Carry a fresh basil leaf in
your purse to ensure it's
always full of notes.

GLAMOUR SPELL
FOR NATURAL ALLURE

A glamour spell helps enhance your natural beauty.

You will need: sugar; a saucer; a lipstick.

1 Sprinkle a circle of sugar on a saucer and pop your favourite lipstick in the middle. Sugar is used to sweeten and attract in magic, and the circle is a symbol of completion and success.

2 Leave for at least an hour.

3 When you apply the lipstick say, 'I apply this lipstick to my lips, with every smile, I do bewitch'.

BE MORE WITCH

Wear a piece of rose quartz close to your heart and you'll have admirers falling at your feet. This stone, associated with Venus, the Roman goddess of love and beauty, is imbued with her powers!

WITCHY MANTRAS

BE YOU, BE-WITCH!

MAGIC IS SOMETHING YOU MAKE.

BELIEVE IT AND IT WILL BE.

EMPOWER, ENCHANT, ENJOY!

MAKE
NATURE
YOUR
GURU

> **'Look deep into nature, and then you will understand everything better.'**
>
> ### ALBERT EINSTEIN

Move over Beyoncé/J.Lo/RiRi, there's a new diva in town and she's unstoppable. Make way for Mother Nature, queen of reinvention. With the power of creation at her fingertips, and a sense of feral freedom, this chick moves with the tides. She makes the best of every season change, while rocking earthy shades with attitude. Whether she's bathed in the super-hot rays of summer, or shivering under winter's alabaster cloak, Mother Nature is beautiful, and a force to be reckoned with. It's no wonder the witches of the world bow to her majesty. After all, she's been here since the beginning of time – that's staying power!

The ancients were also under her spell. They made it their mission to understand and work with her energy, knowing when to plant and tend their crops, and when to take a step back and let the cycles of life do their stuff. They looked to her for inspiration and answers, and she rewarded them with everything they needed to survive. Mother Nature is always supportive.

A muse for artists and writers, guardian of wildlife, wise sage, protector and provider; like most women she juggles many roles, and she does it all with style. This is why every witch worth her salt has her as an ally and friend, and luckily, you don't have to use social media to connect. She is everywhere.

WITCHY WAYS TO GET IN TOUCH WITH MOTHER NATURE

👁 Connect with the environment. Go for a stroll in the park, take the dog for a walk (if you have one!) or potter in the garden.

👁 Get green-fingered. If you don't have a garden you can still grow plants, flowers, herbs and veggies in pots. Getting your hands dirty puts you in direct contact with earth energy.

👁 Engage your senses. When outside, take everything in. Look, hear, feel, smell and taste your surroundings.

👁 Talk to a tree. Find a tree you like and sit with your back against the trunk. Breathe in and notice how it supports you. When you're ready, tell it a secret or reveal a wish – out loud or in your head.

👁 Be creative. Whether you're a budding poet, artist or enjoy crafting, let the land be your muse and make something that reflects the natural beauty of your surroundings.

'All the trees
are losing their
leaves, and not
one of them is
worried.'

DONALD MILLER

THE ENERGY OF LIFE

Witches believe that every living thing is made up of
energy. All of Mother Nature's gifts, from the stones
under foot, to the flowers, plants and trees, have a spirit,
which can be harnessed in a positive way.

BE MORE WITCH

Get to know the plants and flowers in your garden, and how you can use them in spells. Many herbs and flowers have medicinal uses and they're easy to grow. Experiment and have fun creating your own lotions and potions!

ROSEMARY PICK-ME-UP POTION FOR CLARITY AND SUCCESS

Known as the witch's herb, because of its strength; wherever you find rosemary growing, you'll find a powerful woman!

You will need: a handful of fresh rosemary; some boiling water; half a lemon; some honey.

1 Pop the rosemary in a mug and pour in boiling water.

2 Let it steep for five minutes.

3 Strain the water into a glass, then squeeze in the juice of half a lemon.

4 Stir in a spoonful of honey to sweeten.

5 As you stir, see yourself brimming with confidence and ready to take on the world. Then sip slowly.

BE MORE WITCH

Harness the magic of Mother Nature
by growing your own. There is nothing
more miraculous than watching a seed
sprout into a perfect plant. Nurture
and care for your garden, whether
it is indoors or out.

'One touch of nature makes the whole world kin.'

WILLIAM SHAKESPEARE

GET BACK TO NATURE

Tap into Mother Nature's divine lusciousness by giving yourself a makeover. We're not talking catwalk weird, as in dressing in plants and fauna (unless you really want to). Instead take a walk in the countryside and get fashion inspo from the environment.

✧ Include natural shades in your wardrobe, think fern greens, emeralds and sage, amber, gold and soft pinks. Go for a range of hues that match each season.

✧ Look for fabrics with natural patterns; anything from florals to leafy prints, tree or even animal designs, will help you feel connected to the earth.

✧ Give accessories a makeover. Acorns, feathers and crystals make gorgeous pendants. Alternatively, seek out jewellery in the style of these things or opt for wooden beads and necklaces.

✧ Take in the scent of nature and how it makes you feel, then follow your nose and find a perfume that matches the fragrance or make your own using essential oils from plants and flowers.

BE MORE WITCH

Invest in a bottle of rose water,
and spray over freshly washed clothes.
The gorgeous scent is thought to
attract love and happiness.

NETTLE HAIR RINSE

✧ For enchanting tresses that are super soft and shiny, take a handful of fresh nettle leaves and soak overnight in hot water.

✧ In the morning remove the leaves and strain the liquid through a sieve.

✧ Rinse hair thoroughly, making sure there's no residue from the shampoo left, then pour over your scalp and massage in a circular motion while picturing your hair strong and shiny.

✧ Leave to soak in for a couple of minutes before completing a final rinse.

✧ Dry, style, and prepare to be admired!

'The mountains
are calling and
I must go.'

JOHN MUIR

IN YOUR ELEMENT

The elements of earth, air, fire and water are essential for those of a witchy persuasion. Work with them to achieve your dreams and make every day magical.

✦ Appreciate each season. Walk in the rain and feel the fresh droplets on your face. Stand at the top of a hill on a blustery day and let the wind cleanse you from head to toe, or bathe in the Sun's energising glow.

✦ Identify what each element means to you. Draw four columns on a piece of paper. Write the name of an element at the top of each column. Below this, list words that spring to mind when you think about it: for example, fire might make you think about the 'Sun', 'Heat,' 'Joy,' and 'Passion'.

✦ Each sign of the zodiac is governed by an element, find out what yours is and how it affects your personality, then work to your strengths. Earth angels tend to be practical, hardworking and grounded. Fire folks are passionate, outgoing and generous. Water babes are romantic and creative, while air chicks are spontaneous and inventive.

BE MORE WITCH

Borrow qualities from each element by
immersing yourself in it. If you'd like
to be more creative, embrace water by
swimming regularly, or, if you'd like
to be more spontaneous, open all your
windows on a windy day and let the
air sweep through your home.

ELEMENTAL RITUALS

Earth Stand barefoot on a patch of grass. Push the soles of your feet into the earth and drop your weight gently into your knees. As you breathe in, imagine invisible roots stretching up into your feet. These roots keep you grounded and strong.

Air Take a feather and waft lightly above your head for a minute. As you do this, imagine a beam of light passing down from the heavens, hitting the top of your head and cloaking you in white light. You should feel a sudden surge of excitement rushing through you.

Fire Light a candle and gaze at the flame. Place both hands on your stomach above your belly button and imagine a flame inside. Feel it growing in size and strength until you can feel the warmth beneath your fingers. This warmth infuses you with vitality and joy.

Water Hold both wrists under the cold tap and let the water flow over them for a couple of minutes. As you do this, close your eyes, breathe deeply and imagine you're standing under a waterfall of light. As the water hits your body, you will feel more relaxed.

WITCHY MANTRAS

TOUCH NATURE - FEEL MAGIC!

MOTHER NATURE RULES.

BE IN THE WORLD, NOT OF IT.

DON'T BE AFRAID OF THE WOODS, BE AFRAID OF THE WITCH!

3

BROOMSTICKS AREN'T JUST FOR CLEANING

'Imagination will often carry us to worlds that never were. But without it we go nowhere.'

CARL SAGAN

Witches love to daydream. Every little task, from mopping the kitchen floor, to doing your washing is an opportunity to escape into a world of fantasy. This might sound flaky, and non-productive to the untrained mystical eye, but it's an essential element of magical practice. Stretching the imagination helps a witch engage with her creative spirit. She dreams big, to achieve big. She might be pushing a wonky trolley along the aisles of the supermarket, but in her head she's up in the clouds, soaring like an eagle over the mountain tops. When she's not packing her broomstick, the Modern Enchantress flies by the seat of her pants and it all starts in her head.

During the witch trials, tales of witches flying on broomsticks were rife. These howling banshees littered the night sky, leaving a trail of destruction in their wake. Flying folklore offers an array of ointments and potions

thought to send you hurtling through the stratosphere, if not physically then at least metaphorically. While herbs and flowers were often tied to brooms to secure a safe flight, this was a matter of preference. Some airborne mistresses burnt herbs like mugwort and passed their broom through the smoke to encourage take off. Rye bread well past its sell-by date was also a popular and somewhat deadly choice. The mould, known as ergot, was hallucinogenic when applied to the skin and another source of these flights of fancy.

Today's witch takes a safer approach, flying as, when and where her imagination dictates. Being both pilot and cabin crew, she knows her destination and how to reach it in style. The delicious art of daydream means she can 'take off' at the drop of a pointy hat, and while she might not use her broomstick in the same way, it's still a sacred tool and a reminder to brush away the cobwebs, clear the decks and take a leap into the unknown should the fancy take hold.

WITCHY WAYS TO STRETCH THE IMAGINATION

👁 Look through fresh eyes. Take an everyday object and describe it in a new way. Have fun and turn it into an ancient magical artefact. Get creative and come up with inventive ways to use it.

👁 Schedule in daydreaming. Just five minutes a day will make a difference. If you're struggling to get started, picture a place you'd like to visit, then see yourself exploring and having fun.

👁 Instead of plumping for your usual choice of book or film, go for something different. Expand your horizons and let friends and family suggest something you wouldn't normally try.

👁 Find a spot you like outside, take in everything you can see, then have a go at re-creating it, either in picture form or by capturing the spirit of the place in a poem or story.

BE MORE WITCH

Witches love the Moon, not only
does it bathe them in super-flattering
luminescence, it's a powerful magical
aid. Make a point of gazing at the Moon
every night, notice how it changes as it
moves through each phase. Invite the
energy of this powerful orb to infuse
you with creativity. A couple of weeks
of regular Moon-gazing will have you
feeling more creative and energised!

'Logic will get
you from A to Z;
imagination will
get you everywhere.'

ALBERT EINSTEIN

LEARN HOW TO FLY

Witches don't believe in limitations. Whether soaring through the night sky on a super-powered stick, or taking charge in a sticky situation, today's witch has a head for heights and the will to take her further than her wildest dreams.

TAKE FLIGHT AND GET TO WHERE YOU WANT TO BE

Wherever you're headed in life, it's a good idea to start with some pre-flight checks:

✦ Are you in the right place? You don't want to get on the wrong flight, or worse still, miss it altogether, so make sure that you're where you need to be. This means in your head too. How are you feeling right now? Relaxed? Stressed? Angry? No one wants an angry, stressed-out pilot, so take a moment and still the mind.

✦ Are you sure about your destination? You might want to be the boss at work, but will it make you happy? Consider where you're headed in every aspect of your life and if it's going to bring you joy.

✦ How are you going to get there and how long will it take? Do you have a route in mind, or are you prepared for diversions? A detour might seem frustrating but could turn a routine flight into an exciting adventure.

✦ Remember, as with all journeys, you can only plan so much. Relax and enjoy the experience.

GET READY FOR TAKEOFF

Strap yourself in and take a deep breath, you're about to find your wings.

✧ Whatever you've set your sights on, you need to make a start. A small step is enough to lift you in the air, whether that's putting forward your case for a promotion at work or learning a new skill.

✧ Amber is the go-to stone for confidence. Carry or wear, and picture yourself winning at life.

✧ It's okay to coast for a while. Come up for air and take in the view. Are you still happy with where you're headed? If not, make the necessary changes.

MAKE
ROOM
WITH A
BROOM.

'A new broom
sweeps clean, but
the old broom
knows the corners.'

IRISH PROVERB

BROOM RITUALS

In ancient times, brooms were carefully crafted from the wood of the birch or ash tree. Thought to represent the balance between male and female energy, the handle being male and the bristles, female, the broom itself was associated with the element of air, hence its status as a magical flying machine. In modern magic, the broom is seen as a cleansing tool, often used to rid a space of negative energy.

While you might prefer your trusty vacuum cleaner when it comes to a deep-down clean, there's something to be said for the old ways. This ritual will assist you in moving forwards, and at the same time boost the mood and help attract a hefty dollop of abundance. Who said cleaning was dull?

STEP ONE

Invest in a broom, or a brush. Leave it outside overnight beneath the light of the Moon to infuse with magical nighttime energy.

STEP TWO

In the morning, use the broom to sweep around the perimeter of your property. If you live in a flat, sweep around the entrance and doors. As you do this imagine you're creating a golden path that leads into your home.

STEP THREE

Once you've covered outside, get to work inside. Take each room and gently sweep around the edges, while continuing to picture the golden path you're creating.

STEP FOUR

When you've finished say, 'Bad energy be gone, from this moment I move on. Good fortune flows to me, bringing swift prosperity!'

BE MORE WITCH

If you're having trouble getting rid of
something from your life, whether it's a
habit you'd like to change, a behaviour
or a negative situation, visualise yourself
sweeping it away!

'Wisdom begins
in wonder.'

SOCRATES

STARS IN YOUR EYES

When a witch looks at the world she sees something magical. It doesn't matter what she's doing, she'll find a way to make it interesting. Sprinkle some stardust in your life with an enchantment that gives everything (even, *yawn* that pile of paperwork gathering dust in your desk drawer), a spellbinding glow.

LUCKY STARDUST CANDLE

Best performed on a Sunday, the day closely associated with the Sun's positive energy.

You will need: a dab of olive oil associated with love and beauty; an orange or yellow candle to represent happiness; a pot of gold glitter.

1 Massage the olive oil into the wax of the candle.

2 Sprinkle the glitter evenly on some paper and roll the candle in it to give an even covering.

3 Light the wick and make the following wish: 'Pretty candle sparkling bright, casting rays of flickering light. Magic is in all I see, beauty found and beauty be.'

4 Let the candle burn down, while giving thanks for all the blessings in your life.

BE MORE WITCH

Every day write a gratitude list. Jot
down everything you're thankful for,
from that first morning brew that fuels
your day, to the comfy pillow where
you rest your head every night. Witches
count their blessings!

WITCHY MANTRAS

IF THE BROOM FITS, RIDE IT.

CAST SPELLS AND DREAMS IN COLOUR.

FIND YOUR WINGS AND USE THEM.

FLY FREE, FLY HIGH, FLY THE BROOMSTICK!

4

SISTERHOOD IS SPELLBINDING

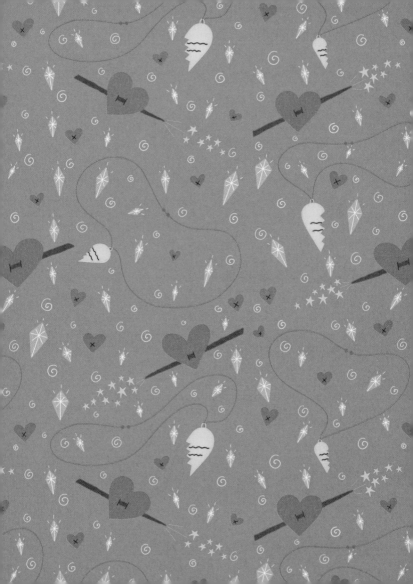

> '**One woman is a tiny divine spark in a timeless sisterhood tapestry collective; all of us are Wild Women.**'

JAN PORTER, *SOUL SKIN*

How many wonderful and inspiring women do you know? The world is full of them and while every woman may not be a witch, every witch is definitely a woman. Together that makes an army of sass that would have a monster, imagined or otherwise, turning on its heel. As any fool who has chanced his arm and tried to stir things up among a group of girlfriends will attest, ladies stick together like glue. Throw magic into the mix, and you've got a winning combination, otherwise known as girrrrrrrrrrrl power!

Mystical babes take friendship to a new level, supporting and nurturing each other at all times. When the going gets tough, these ladies get tougher, working together to achieve the impossible, for in sisterhood lies the

secret of success – witch rule number one. And while you might envisage groups of cackling crones gathered around a bubbling cauldron, these days 'cocktail covens' are *de rigueur*. It's less 'Eye of Newt' and more 'Long Island Iced Tea', when these girls get together. Covens are shaped by their members, meaning it's more about the group's intention than how they look, so never underestimate ladies that lunch, they could be ladies that cast spells!

Witches are powerlifters; not in the literal weightlifting sense, but on a spiritual level – they raise each other up to new heights. With praise and encouragement as the rocket fuel, these ladies reach for the stars. Should they stumble, there's always a soft sisterly landing pad to break the fall, swiftly followed by tea and cake. The general rule is if it isn't fun, it isn't done, so grab your closest girl pals and get your heads together because it's time to roll with the magic!

START YOUR OWN COVEN

A coven is a group that meets regularly, with a common interest in magic. Rites and rituals are performed when they get together, along with celebrating key wiccan festivals throughout the year. Some witches prefer to fly solo, rather than joining an existing coven, but there's no reason why you can't start your own.

✧ Get a group of like-minded friends together. It doesn't have to be big, a coven can be three, or 300!

✧ Set your intentions as a group. What are you going to do when you meet up? Have a catch-up and talk about magic? Share and practise spells? Or simply encourage each other's aspirations? It's your coven, you decide.

✧ Make a commitment. Decide when you're going to meet and for how long, then put it in your diary. Covens work when everyone puts time and energy into them.

✧ Choose the right meeting place. This might vary depending on what you're going to do, so for a general magical catch-up, a wine bar or café works, but for spell-casting some, private space is needed.

BE MORE WITCH

Give each meeting a different theme; for example, you could cover love magic in one session and healing in another. Work to each other's strengths, so if one of you is well versed in folklore, give them the floor for a session, or if you have an expert on the healing properties of plants and flowers, let them share their knowledge.

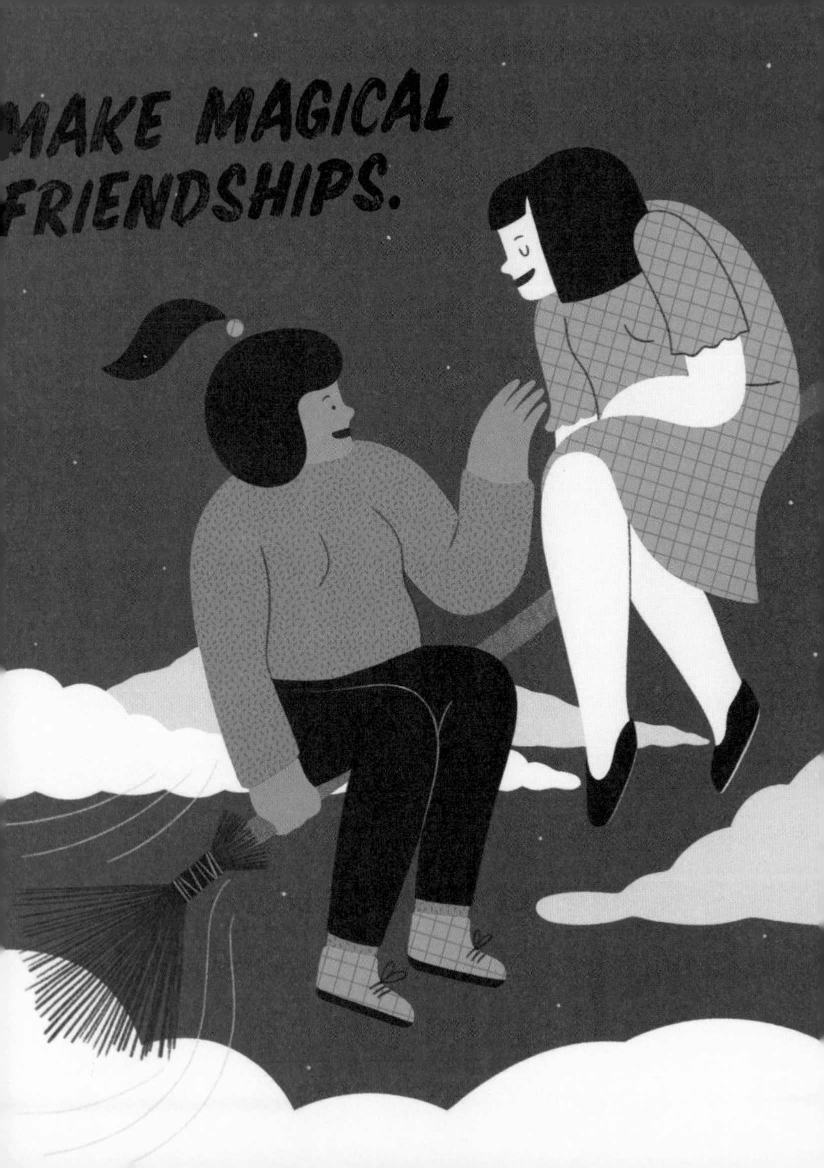
MAKE MAGICAL
FRIENDSHIPS.

'Walking with a friend in the dark is better than walking alone in the light.'

HELEN KELLER

SOUL SISTER SPELL

Strengthen a friendship and send a bumper mystical hug with this spell, which combines the feel-good power of chocolate, with positive energy.

You will need: a pin; a white candle; your favourite bar of milk chocolate.

1 Sacred to the Aztecs, chocolate is often used in spells to create harmony. Milk chocolate will strengthen a friendship, while dark chocolate is best for love spells.

2 Take a pin and carve both of your names into the wax of the candle.

3 Light the candle and place the chocolate in front of it.

4 Bring an image of your friend to mind and imagine giving her a hug.

5 Let the candle burn down, then share the chocolate bar with your friend when you next meet up.

RENEW A FRIENDSHIP RITUAL

With such busy lives, it's easy to lose touch with female friends, but all is not lost. Even if things have turned sour with your sister from another mister, you can renew the bond with this transformation ritual.

✧ Take an ice cube, or if you have access to some snow, that will also do.

✧ Pop it in a dish with a piece of paper with your friend's name on it.

✧ Place near a fire or heater, then watch as the ice gently melts while picturing your friend's smiling face.

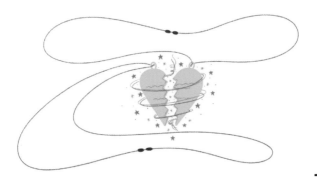

BE MORE WITCH

Ice is a versatile magic ingredient.
It can be used when you need to put
something on ice – for example, a
disagreement or an argument that
won't go away. Just write a few words
to sum up the situation, pop in a
freezer bag and fill with water.
Stick this in your freezer and chill!

LIGHT
THE DIVINE
SPARK.

'A woman in sync
with her power can
change the world.'

SHIKOBA

UNLEASH YOUR INNER GODDESS

Big on feminine energy, a witch knows that she's a wonder woman in every respect. She taps into her inner goddess daily and draws on this super power to achieve her goals.

STEP ONE
Stand with your feet hip-width apart, your shoulders relaxed and breathe deeply. Place both hands over the middle of your chest with your palms down.

STEP TWO
Stretch your arms open and outwards as if you're embracing the space in front of you.

STEP THREE
Take a deep breath in. As you breathe out, pull your hands back into your chest, palms together as if in prayer.

STEP FOUR
Say, in a loud confident voice, 'I unleash my inner goddess, I harness the power within!'

TOP FIVE MYSTICAL BABES

Whether you're looking for motivation, creativity or a quick confidence boost, these mythical chicks have all the attitude and magical know-how you'll need.

Hecate
Greek goddess of witches and women. Firm but fair, she'll help you stand your ground and overcome challenging obstacles.

Bast
Egyptian goddess and protector of cats and women, known for her love of music and dance. She'll help you express yourself and find your voice.

Freya
Norse goddess of love, beauty and war. Leader of a kick-ass tribe of women known as the Valkyries. Call on her for courage and charm.

Ceridwen
Celtic mother goddess and keeper of the cauldron of wisdom. This powerful enchantress assists in all matters of magic and can give your spells the edge!

BE MORE WITCH

Make a goddess altar. Clear a shelf or coffee table, then choose a deity. Get to know her better by finding out her attributes; goddesses often have flowers, stones, scents and symbols associated with them, so include their favourites on your altar, along with any written requests or wishes.

REAL WITCHES FIX EACH OTHER'S BROOMS.

OWN YOUR POWER, UNLEASH YOUR LIGHT.

WHEN WOMEN COME TOGETHER MAGIC HAPPENS.

KEEP YOUR FRIENDS CLOSE, AND YOUR COVEN CLOSER.

5

NEVER BE
AFRAID TO
VENTURE
INTO THE
FOREST

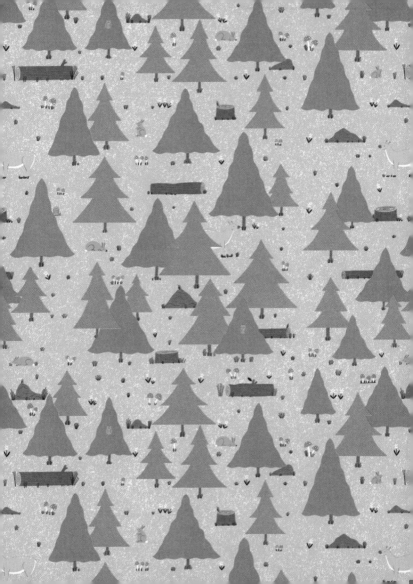

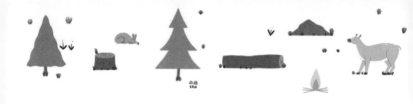

'I am not afraid of storms, for I'm learning how to sail my ship.'

LOUISA MAY ALCOTT

Witches laugh in the face of fear, and we're not talking high-pitched cackles. Your average enchantress doesn't scare easily. She knows that feeling the fear is one thing, but succumbing to it is another. Being the subject of many horror tales down the ages, a witch understands that by far the scariest thing in life is letting fear control you. It is much braver to step out of your comfort zone, look the monster in the eye and be mistress of your own fate.

While this attitude might seem a tad devil-may-care, this is not about taking risks. A witch picks her battles, sticks to her principles and remains sole commander and captain of her ship. She is comfortable in her own skin, confident in her abilities, and knows that come what may she will prevail. The Ferris wheel of life keeps moving, so even at the lowest point, the wheel is turning and a new day awaits. This knowledge is enough to restore calm when things get mystically iffy, which they do (even for the most practised witch) from time to time. Needless to say, the savvy sorceress always has a few tips and tricks up her sleeve to deal with a crisis.

'You gain strength, courage and confidence by every experience in which you really stop to look fear in the face.'

ELEANOR ROOSEVELT

WITCHY FEAR FIXERS

Supercharge your courage with these magically inspired tips.

👁 The pentagram is the witch's symbol of protection. It can be traced, drawn or visualised to help you feel strong and grounded.

👁 Imagine a thread of light running through the centre of your body. It gently tugs and lengthens your spine, while pulling you in at the core. Maintain this strong posture to feel in control.

👁 Breathe deeply. Count each breath in and out to four beats, then extend by one. You'll take in more oxygen, which calms anxiety and helps you feel mentally alert.

👁 Imagine a witch's cloak of protection draped over your shoulders shielding you from negative energy and hurtful words.

BE MORE WITCH

Ask the Greek goddess Hecate for her support. This kick-ass deity, also known as the Queen of the Witches, is not to be trifled with. Call out her name and ask for assistance.

'Nothing in life is to be feared, it is only to be understood. Now is the time to understand more, so that we may fear less.'

MARIE CURIE

CREATE A CIRCLE OF POWER

A circle of power is a safe place, from which you can work magic spells. It can be a physical circle, marked out in some way or an imagined space, depending on personal preference. You can create one, anytime and anywhere, so you never have to feel vulnerable again.

STEP ONE

Decide where you'd like your space to be and how you're going to mark it out; for example, by placing a circular rug, using stones, or visualising a ring of light.

STEP TWO

Stand in the centre of the circle and picture a shower of light bathing you and the space in positive energy. This light will cleanse the area of any residual negativity.

STEP THREE

For extra protection imagine a Teflon dome surrounding you. Nothing sticks to this wall, so hurtful words or emotions rebound from it like water off a duck's back.

BE MORE WITCH

Make your workspace a sanctuary.
Visualise a circle of fire around yourself
to keep troublesome colleagues, course
mates or family members at a safe
distance. Adjust the flames in your
mind, so when you need to retreat,
you're well protected and when you're
open to communication, you can
turn down the heat.

A FAMILIAR STORY

In the Middle Ages it was commonly believed that witches could take on other shapes and forms, usually while under attack or fleeing the scene of a crime. From a feral feline to a large black dog, the average spell-worker was fleet of foot and furry. Cats, in particular, were their vessel of choice, being creatures of the night with an air of mystery and a penchant for getting into mischief. What's more, without the invention of Louis Vuitton or Gucci, these magical moggies were also the accessory of choice for those with a mystical bent. Classed as familiars, and able to commune with the spirit world, cats were the Twitter of the time, keeping their mistresses up-to-date on the latest magical gossip and acting as a portal to the fairy world.

Today we understand more about cats and witches and appreciate folklore for what it is. Nevertheless, every witch needs a cat or three to keep her company, and if not, an army of furry and feathered friends on hand from which she can draw strength and peace during times of stress.

WITCHY WAYS TO CONNECT WITH ANIMAL MAGIC

✧ If you already have a pet, set aside an allotted time each day and devote it to them. From playing and stroking to simply sitting with your pet, you'll feel stronger and calmer in their company, and they'll appreciate the love.

✧ Borrow a furry friend. From walking a friend's dog, to being kind to neighbourhood cats, there are lots of ways you can connect with the animal world and reap the benefits.

✧ Fill your home with pictures of the animals you admire, particularly those with the qualities you aspire to. This will help you connect with their energy.

BE MORE WITCH

Learn how to communicate with your
familiar. Look into their eyes, send all
your love, then ask them how they feel.
You may see an image, a word, or get
an overwhelming feeling. Don't worry
if nothing happens at first, it takes time
and practice to establish a connection,
so keep trying.

'Never let the fear
of striking out get
in your way.'

BABE RUTH

USE YOUR FEARS

Witches do; they don't dally or hide away. They may be scared, but ultimately, they use this to their advantage as a force to drive them forwards. It's this 'witch-attude' that helps them soar to new heights, with or without their trusty broom.

GET WISE, GET
WITCH-ATTUDE!

1 Whatever fear you're facing, ask yourself, 'What is the worst that can happen and how likely is this?'

2 Then ask if there's anything you can do to stop this from happening, or are matters out of your control?

3 If the reality of the fear is not as bad as you first thought, let it go.

4 If the fear is unlikely to happen, let it go.

5 If it's out of your control, let it go.

6 If there's something you can do, take control and act.

SPELL TO BANISH FEAR

This spell is best performed on the night of a full Moon.

You will need: a pen; a sheet of paper; a black candle; a fireproof bowl; a pot with some soil, or access to a garden.

1 Think of a symbol or a couple of words to describe your fear and write this down. As you do, imagine you're pouring your anxiety into the paper.

2 Light the black candle.

3 Fold the paper and pass it through the flame, then drop it in the bowl.

4 Watch as the fear burns, then take the ashes and bury them deep in the soil. As you do this say, 'This fear is vanquished by fire and flame. Back to the earth, from whence it came'.

WITCHY MANTRAS

LEAP AND YOU`LL FLY!

TURN FEAR INTO FASCINATION.

FEEL THE FEAR, THEN VANQUISH IT.

BE WHAT YOU WANT TO BE.

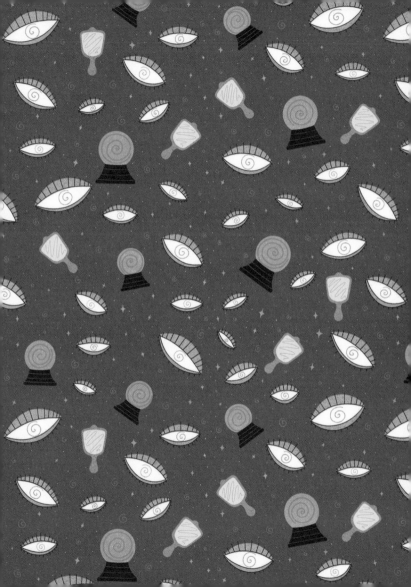

'The more you trust your intuition, the more empowered you become, the stronger you become, and the happier you become.'

GISELË BUNDCHEN

Witches have all the answers. This is not because they think they know it all. They do, simple as. Intuition is their BFF and gives them everything they need to succeed. Psychic skills go hand in hand with magic, and most who practise the craft have a keen interest in all things divinatory. This is because a finely tuned sixth sense is as much a part of the witch's toolkit as her wand or cauldron. Whether she's creating spells, manifesting the future or putting up shelves, it's the glue that makes everything fit. It can cause jitters if something feels off kilter, or an excited buzz in the pit of the stomach that suggests adventure is afoot. Whatever form it takes, a good witch learns to listen to it, just as she would her best bud.

That's not to say that the future is set in stone and can only be predicted. A savvy sorceress makes things happen, her way. Destiny doesn't dabble, preferring to keep a safe distance and let her get on with conjuring the perfect path. After all, mystical or not, we're all different. There's no one size fits all when it comes to life and how you live it. Although there's a strong tradition of magical practitioners throughout the ages using tarot cards and crystal balls to predict the future, the visions and insights they reveal are just a snapshot of what could potentially be. Free will overrides the hoodoo, should you wish to change the outcome. In other words, go girl, you've got this!

MAKE INTUITION YOUR BFF

There's a reason why they say trust your gut instinct. The stomach is one of the first areas to physically channel intuition, from getting butterflies when you're anticipating excitement to feeling tight when things aren't right. A wise witch looks after her tum and listens when it speaks!

STEP ONE

Place both hands over your solar plexus, the area above your belly button. Breathe steadily and picture an orange ball of light filling the space with warmth.

STEP TWO

Feel the warmth spread throughout your stomach and into the rest of your body. Enjoy this sensation of being perfectly at ease and take note of any thoughts or feelings that arise during this period.

STEP THREE

Practise every day and you'll notice when your stomach is telling you something other than 'Feed me now!'

GET
THE
LOOK.

'There is a voice
that doesn't use
words, listen.'

RUMI

WITCHY WAYS TO HARNESS YOUR SIXTH SENSE

👁 Hold a piece of amethyst, thought to boost psychic power, it's a pretty accessory too!

👁 The universe works in signs and symbols, so keep a lookout for synchronicities. For example, you might have been thinking of hitting the gym but fear is holding you back. A leaflet for a new class lands at your feet, a sign from the universe that means, 'Go for it!'

👁 Pay attention to your dreams. Write down what you can remember on waking. It might not make much sense, but over time you could see a clear pattern developing.

👁 Test yourself. The next time your phone rings or pings with text, don't check to see who it's from, guess! Say the first thing that comes into your head. The more you practise the more your sixth sense kicks in and your psychic super powers improve.

JUST BE MORE WITCH

Practise your intuitive skills with a spot of tea leaf reading – don't worry, if coffee's your brew, you can read the grains!

✧ Sip and ask for an insight into the future.

✧ Leave a dribble of liquid at the bottom with the leaves/grains. Swirl around the cup three times, then turn over onto the saucer.

✧ Flip it back over quickly and look for any symbols or patterns that have a hidden meaning.

✧ To decipher, think about what the symbol means to you; for example, something that looks like a pen might suggest an urge to express yourself, or simply that you've got some emails and letters to catch up on.

✧ Popular symbols include the Sun or star for happy times ahead; coins which indicate a cash windfall; an arrow suggesting you're moving forwards; a boat or plane which indicates a journey.

'Seeing is believing, but feeling's the truth.'

THOMAS FULLER

EYE SPY

Mothers and witches have something in common.
Aside from being super powerful and wise, they also
have eyes in the back of their heads!

Not strictly true in the literal sense, but the third eye
chakra is an energy centre located in the middle of the
forehead. This invisible eye helps you connect intuitively
to the subconscious mind, and other supernatural
realms. Those adept in working with it can see, sense
and annoyingly anticipate what you're going to do
before the thought comes into your mind. Mums do
this naturally, being closely connected to their offspring,
but those of a witchy persuasion also know how to
power it up.

THIRD EYE PSYCHIC POWER SPELL

You will need: a purple candle; some lavender essential oil; a bowl of warm water.

1 Purple is the colour associated with psychic perception, so start by lighting the candle to create the right atmosphere.

2 Add five drops of lavender essential oil to a small bowl of warm water. Breathe in the sweet aroma, then dip your finger into the liquid.

3 Swirl your finger through the liquid and repeat this magical chant, 'Third eye open, third eye see, what is meant, and what will be'.

4 When you've finished, imagine you're looking at a cinema screen inside your head. Let any images, patterns or words appear.

BE MORE WITCH

The third eye is like a psychic antenna and can be turned on at any time by visualising a small purple flower bud in the centre of the forehead. Imagine the petals slowly unfurling to reveal a bright ball of purple light.

'Nothing can dim the light that shines from within.'

MAYA ANGELOU

THE EYES HAVE IT

Being the windows of the soul, and therefore a portal to the imagination and our deepest desires, the eyes definitely have it! In other words, it pays to look after your peepers! Check out these mystical eyes of note and tap into their power.

THE EYE OF RA

The Ancient Egyptians knew their stuff; when protecting themselves and their loved ones, they turned to the Eye of Ra. Associated with the Sun god of the same name, it's also a representation of a number of goddesses. All powerful, this mystic eye sees everything!

Try this:
Draw the Eye of Ra on a piece of paper, then leave beneath a doormat, or near the entrance to your home to protect all who enter. You can also infuse beauty essentials with a burst of sunlight, by popping the same symbol into your make-up bag!

TIGER'S EYE

With striking bands of gold, this eye-catching crystal has many magical uses. Its vibrant energy provides balance and strength and wearing the stone can alleviate anxiety.

Try this:
For a powerful facial that brightens, make a tiger's eye infusion. Leave the stone in a bowl of water overnight. Remove in the morning and soak a flannel in the liquid. Squeeze away excess water then place the flannel over you face for five minutes. Relax and feel the invigorating energy of the crystal seeping into your skin.

DRAGON'S EYE

Mighty and magnificent, dragons blaze a trail through folklore. It was thought that you could see into the heart of the beast by gazing into its eyes. A symbol of courage, love and infinite wisdom, dragon's eyes will get you noticed for all the right reasons!

Try this:
If you like to experiment with colour, give your make-up a fiery hue and opt for a gold-tinted eyeshadow. If *au naturel* is more your thing, just apply a spot of moisturiser, and gently massage around each eye while picturing the golden orb of a dragon's eye.

BE MORE WITCH

For enchanting eyes, make fennel your go-to herb. Brew a tea using the fresh leaves, or a shop-bought tea bag. Let it cool, then use as an eye wash. Your peepers will thank you for it!

WITCHY MANTRAS

LISTEN TO YOUR INNER WITCH.

———

REACH BEYOND WHAT YOU CAN SEE.

———

YOU ARE EVERYTHING YOU NEED.

———

TRUST, BELIEVE, CONJURE!

'It's important to remember that we all have magic inside of us.'

J.K. ROWLING

You are magic; something every witch recognises and celebrates. Magic isn't a separate entity. It lives inside you and works through your thoughts, intentions and deeds. You are it. It starts with you, and while you might struggle with the idea that you have the potential for greatness, let me assure you – you do. As a divine being you are unique and gifted in a myriad of ways. You might refuse to see this and instead fixate on superficial things, like your ample (and rather glorious) derrière or the fresh cluster of pimples on your nose, but we on the other side of the looking glass, have an altogether different view.

It's simple. A witch, does not sweat, perspire or even glow about the little things. In typical high-spirited fashion, she prefers to fly with her flaws, shouting

from her broomstick, 'Look at me, I'm perfect as I am!' Yes, she has anxieties and there are things she'd like to change, but on the whole, on the surface and much deeper, she's a damn fine creation and fabulous specimen of womanhood. Being different isn't something to be maligned. It's called being you.

Consider those wise women of old, the sages, herbalists, medicine women and all-round voodoo queens gracing every corner of the world. The fact that their faces were lined with age and seasoned by the Sun was not important. These matriarchs were respected for their wisdom, for the essence of knowledge that flowed through their veins. Their uniqueness was rejoiced wholeheartedly. So, listen up ladies of the broom, true magic, in its purest and most powerful form, comes from the heart. It manifests in the way you move, talk, interact and live. Once you accept and love who you are, the magic flows.

'To love oneself
is the beginning
of a lifelong
romance.'

OSCAR WILDE

WITCHY WAYS TO LOVE YOURSELF

👁 Make a list of all the things you like about yourself. Consider physical qualities, character traits, skills and talents. When you run out of things, ask your family and friends for their input. Read the list and add to it, regularly.

👁 Celebrate successes, big and small. When you've achieved something, whether it's a pile of washing, finishing an important essay or just getting through a difficult meeting, give yourself a pat on the back.

👁 Go on a date with yourself. Don't save that fancy restaurant or movie for when you have company, treat yourself. Learn to enjoy alone time and appreciate just how magical you are.

👁 Do what makes you happy. Relax and have fun, whether that's kicking up the dance floor, or soaking in a luxurious scented bath. You deserve it!

'Everyone's a star
and deserves the
right to twinkle.'

MARILYN MONROE

SELF-ESTEEM SPELL

Having an off day? Don't despair, this magical morsel will have you flying high in no time.

You will need: a yellow tea light; a saucer; a couple of petals from a sunflower or a handful of sunflower seeds, associated with the Sun and radiating joy; a piece of citrine, an uplifting stone known as the 'cuddle quartz'; a sprig of rosemary for personal power.

1 Light the tea light and place a saucer in front of it. Put the sunflower petals or seeds in the saucer. Then place the citrine in the centre of the saucer before finally adding in the sprig of rosemary.

2 Chant the following words, 'I am fabulous, I am free. I enjoy being me. As this charm will attest, I am always at my best.' Repeat while the candle burns down.

3 To finish pop all the ingredients in a charm bag, or wrap in a handkerchief and tie the ends together. Keep this magical parcel with you for the next three days to increase in confidence and joy.

BE MORE WITCH

Sunflower seeds are the magical snack
of choice. They're packed with powerful
nutrients and eating them is thought
to attract abundance! Munch while
thinking happy thoughts!

'Kind words can be short and easy to speak but their echoes are truly endless.'

MOTHER TERESA

AS EASY AS ONE, TWO, THREE…

A little number crunching goes a long way in the magical world. Witches have a thing for the power of three. This number represents aspects of the triple goddess, the maiden, the mother and the crone, all important and equally kick-ass phases of womanhood. Three also comes in to play with spells, and it's a common belief that whatever you put out, you get back threefold. This explains why kindness is top of the witchy agenda, along with compassion and a generous dollop of good humour. Together these make the perfect balance of ingredients for a magnificently magical existence!

ENCHANTING WAYS TO SPREAD KINDNESS

✦ Give compliments freely. Find something nice to say to at least one person a day and watch their face glow with joy.

✦ Make a wish for someone else. If you know someone is struggling or think they could do with a boost, take a deep breath, picture them looking happy and wish them good fortune, in your mind or out loud!

✦ Offer a helping hand. Whether you're holding the door open for someone, carrying shopping or just giving advice, go out of your way to be kind.

✦ Bake a cake. Recipes are spells for the stomach. Like any type of magic, a good one has the power to make you feel instantly happier. Make some cakes and as they bake imagine you're infusing them with love, then share with family and friends.

'I've been searching for ways to heal myself, and I've found that kindness is the best way.'

LADY GAGA

HEAL YOURSELF, HEAL THE WORLD

Use your mystical super powers to heal nearest and dearest, or those further afield in three easy steps.

STEP ONE
Imagine you're standing in a cleansing circle of white light.

STEP TWO
If you have a picture of the person you'd like to heal, hold it in your hands. If you want to send out healing energy to the world, bring an image of planet Earth to mind.

STEP THREE
Imagine the image dowsed in blue paint. Take this a step further and imagine you're also covered from head to toe in blue. This shade is associated with healing, and soothes pain and anxiety too, so wearing it or immersing yourself in it helps when you're feeling under the weather. The more healing energy you send out, the more you'll receive – you can't lose!

BE MORE WITCH

In folklore, yellow flowers lift the spirits
and bring healing energy into the home.
Also renowned for attracting fairies,
they'll provide an instant burst of
sunshine. Pop a vase of yellow blooms in
your living room, open the window and
invite fey magic into your life!

BANISH WORRY
TO THE BIN SPELL

Worry not! It holds you back, feeds insecurities and makes you feel bad. Having said that, it's a part of life and hard to eliminate completely. If you find your worries getting on top of you, try this ritual.

You will need: a potato; a peeler; a bin!

1 Governed by the Moon, potatoes have a reassuring energy which explains why they're one of our favourite comfort foods.

2 Hold a potato in both hands above an open bin. Say, 'I cast away my worries now, my fears and doubts are gone. This burden has been lifted, and now I can move on.'

3 Peel the potato and let the shavings drop in the bin. As you do this, imagine you're peeling away layers of worry to reveal a lighter, brighter version of yourself.

BE MORE WITCH

The same ritual can be used to remove
anything from your life, so if there's
a bad habit you'd like to ditch or an
annoying ex hanging around, perform
the above and replace 'my worries'
with 'this problem'.

MAGICAL + ENCHANTING = ME!

FLY WITH YOUR FLAWS.

WOMAN FIRST, WITCH ALWAYS.

SPREAD KINDNESS LIKE STARDUST, CAST SPELLS WITH LOVE.

WITCH'S CREED

A WITCH ALWAYS...

BELIEVES that something magical is about to happen

BELIEVES that anything is possible

BELIEVES in what she feels

BELIEVES in herself

Publishing Director Sarah Lavelle
Editor Harriet Butt
Editorial Assistant Harriet Webster
Designer Katherine Keeble
Illustrator Megan Reddi
Production Director Vincent Smith
Production Controller Tom Moore

Published in 2019 by Quadrille,
an imprint of Hardie Grant Publishing

Quadrille
52–54 Southwark Street
London SE1 1UN
quadrille.com

Cataloguing in Publication Data:
a catalogue record for this book
is available from the British Library.

text © Alison Davies 2019
illustrations © Megan Reddi 2019
design © Quadrille 2019

ISBN 978 1 78713 338 9

Printed in China